I WANNA TELL YOU A FUNNY STORY

MAX BYGRAVES

Illustrations by Barry Green

To my wife Blossom
who said to me in the kitchen one day,
'You keep getting in the way –
go and write a book!'

First published in Great Britain in 1992 by Robson Books Ltd, Bolsover House, 5-6 Clipstone Street, London W1P 7EB

Text copyright © 1992 Max Bygraves
Illustrations copyright © 1992 Barry Green
The right of Max Bygraves to be identified as author of this work has been asserted by him in accordance with the Copyright, Designs and Patents Act 1988

British Library Cataloguing in Publication Data
A catalogue record for this book is available from the British Library

ISBN 0 86051 824 8

Typeset by Spectrum Typesetting Ltd., London
Printed and bound in Great Britain by
Butler & Tanner Ltd, Frome and London

INTRODUCTION

We were sitting in a small café near Leicester Square. Solly, my agent, was finishing off ten per cent of my cheesecake, when I casually mentioned that when some recording artistes pass on they seem to sell more records then when they were alive — I was thinking of Elvis Presley, Jim Reeves, Buddy Holly — 'I wonder if it will happen to me?' Quick as a flash, Solly said, 'Let's give it a try'.

He can become most disagreeable at a refusal. I remember the time, years ago, when he called me — all excited. 'I've just had a movie offer for you to play the part of Long John Silver in Treasure Island — it's ten thousand pounds a week, twelve weeks' shooting in the Bahamas — all expenses paid ....' I told him it would be wonderful, I'd do it. He said, 'How do you feel about a leg amputation?' When I refused, he said, 'We could get away with it, just below the knee'. Again I said no and he sulked for a week.

His latest brain wave was, '*We* should write a book.' Whenever there's work to be done it's always 'we', he contributes very little but most of the time it's '*we*'. If he comes to a theatre where I have worked on an audience to receive an ovation, Solly will be in the wings smiling as I exit — 'Hey! We were terrific tonight — weren't *we?*' If I have an off night or the audience are not so receptive, he'd say, 'What happened to *you?*'

He convinced me that if I probed the old memory box, I'd find a book ready to be written. I paid the bill, we parted, I made my way to my apartment in Westminster. I decided to stroll through St James's Park trying to come to grips with Solly's suggestion about writing a book, but all I could think of was, '...why are birds and animals allowed to poop all over the footpaths and yet if we did the same, we'd finish up at Cannon Row Police Station?'

Solly's words kept coming back: 'Write a book — linger

over your childhood days – that always sells – make it a sort of Bermondsey Revisited, mention the poverty – get to the heart strings – you can do it Max ... and leave the syndication rights to me!'

I sat down on a bench next to a dear old lady feeding the sparrows. 'Aren't the birds lovely?' I said. She gathered her things together and with a 'Sod off, pervert!' she went. I began wishing I hadn't worn my old raincoat – I took it off, put it over my arm and carried on walking in the autumn drizzle, wishing I was wearing thermals. Solly and the book was still on my mind so I decided to invest in a writing pad at a shop opposite Buckingham Palace stables. Alone in my flat, my wife had gone to Harrods sale. I remember it well: she came in all excited to tell me she had bought some great bargains: Two pairs of sheets, a cheese grater, a china rolling pin and a hovercraft. Honestly, twenty-one miles of English Channel and she backs into the Isle of Wight.

But now I was alone with pad and pencil and all those years to look back on ...

Born Free! That's because my mother couldn't afford anything else – she got Mrs Lyons next door to do the midwife bit and I made an entrance weighing nine and a quarter pounds, a great relief to my nineteen-year-old mother who had tried to pretend for almost six months prior to my birth that I was a blind boil.

The women around the Bermondsey area had large families, sometimes fourteen kids – some of those women hadn't seen their feet for more than a dozen years.

There was no family planning or contraception in those days, no such thing as the Pill, the nearest thing to the Pill was Beechams Pills – 'take six of those last thing at night and you're never in bed long enough for anything to happen', that was the theory among the women that didn't want to 'fall'. Condoms were too expensive for the unemployed and there were so many of these poor blokes 'bomping on' for the dole, a luxury like a condom was out of the question.

4

My father brought a condom home once and placed it on the table. 'What's that?' asked my mother. 'It's what you asked me to get at the shops,' said Dad. She sighed, 'No; I said if you are passing the shops bring back a *FRESH LETTUCE!'*

Consequently, during the following years, she gave birth to six little Bygraves; my sister Kath was the puny one – she only weighed eight and a quarter pounds. Nine of us, including our grandfather, lived in a two-room council flat that cost eight shillings and fourpence rent per week – when they got it.

Nowadays, you can walk through the streets of London in summer and outside cafés there are tables and chairs – we had the same thing in our district – but in those days they called it *eviction*.

Money was scarce but seemed to go further – lifting five shillings' worth of groceries could give you a hernia – and the only nasal decongestant was your little finger. If you said, 'Is it a boy or a girl?' you were usually looking at a baby, and a 'bra' was a nightwatchman's coke fire.

So this was the environment yours truly spent the first seventeen years of a life in – saved by the war, which seems to shock quite a few when I tell them it was the best thing that happened for me. Sure, like thousands of others I hated the bombs and the nights spent huddled up in air raid shelters, no food in the shops and the spartan existence, but at seventeen I joined up in the RAF and for the first time saw a wide new world, it was the first time I ever spent a night in a bed by myself. The first morning I woke up and found I was alone, I thought I was dead.

I had a secret weapon for existence, I had it then and have it now, it was defence against the cruel world. I would try to make people laugh – it's a great ploy because a man will never hit or pick a fight with a bloke that makes him laugh. As soon as I got into uniform and for almost five more years, I learned how to tell a 'story' and raise a smile – no good if you met the enemy face to face, especially at seventeen, 'cos I didn't know too many German jokes, but there were quite a few Gestapo types to contend with on British soil and I managed to get through those war years unscathed. In my RAF uniform, I was equal to thousands of others, but with a 'story' or two, I began to be sought after – that's how I became a story teller and the rewards have been extraordinary.

I have strolled some of the great fairways of the world partnering golfers such as Bobby Locke, Seve Ballesteros, Greg Norman, Tony Jacklin and quite a few other world champions. I have shared the stage with almost all the great names of show business – nineteen Royal Variety Performances, thirty-one gold discs for millions of best selling albums, television, radio, Broadway, private lunch with HM Queen Elizabeth II, awarded the OBE ... Hey, wait a minute Max, get back to Solly and the book.

Oh yes, on the following pages are some 'stories' I have lived on. Some are by writers, some told at the golf club. Some by colleagues and some I made up, but all of them got big laughs so it's horses for courses, but whether you are in the locker room or at the vicar's tea party, there's a story here that will suit. My little pen portraits of friends are all true.

Cheers!

Max Bygraves

An old convict has a group of young convicts around him and asks what they did to get put inside.

1ST CON.:   I got done for housebreaking.

OLD CON.:   How many d'ye get for that?

1ST CON.:   Seven years.

2ND CON.:   I'm in for bank robbery.

OLD CON.:   How many d'ye get for that?

2ND CON.:   Ten years.

3RD CON.:   A water pistol got me in 'ere.

OLD CON.:   How could a water pistol get you in here?

3RD CON.:   When I was on the outside, I had this water pistol, I used to fill it up with petrol and I'd go round looking for punk rockers – I don't like punk rockers – so I would squirt this petrol over 'em then throw a lighted match on 'em....

OLD CON.:   How many d'ye get for that?

3RD CON.:   About sixteen to the gallon!

When the train robbers were caught they got heavy sentences, some as many as thirty years.

The story goes that one of the wives wrote to her husband inside telling him that the back garden was overgrown and because he was away for thirty years, she was thinking of digging up the whole of the garden and planting potatoes.

Of course, the mail going out of prison is mostly censored and as some of the loot from the robbery had never been found, the police became interested when the jailbird wrote back to his wife saying, 'Whatever you do –*don't* dig up the back garden'.

Several days later, another letter arrived from the wife who wrote, 'There were three CID men and sixteen uniformed policemen here today and they dug up the whole of the back garden'.

The fellow inside wrote back, 'Now plant the potatoes'.

A young fellow arrives from America and goes to a cemetery just outside London where he asks if he can see his grandfather's grave.

'What was your grandfather's name?'

'Smith, John Smith'.

'Oh dear, we've got quite a few John Smiths here – could you be more specific?'

'Well', says the young American, '... during the 1950s he was crossword champion of Great Britain'.

'That may help – let's have a look at the records – um – um – oh yes – here we are, John Smith – Crossword Champion United Kingdom 1948 – 1953' (pointing at graves) 'he's nine down and five across!'

TOMMY COOPER

Tommy and I started in show business about the same time, just after the war. We had both served in the forces for almost five years, him with the army, me with the RAF. We were both uncertain in which direction to go. Believe it or not he was quite serious about his conjuring tricks and at that time hardly ever spoke during his act – he let the tricks earn the applause.

My act was made up mostly of singing impressions, singers like Hutch, the Ink Spots and a few others currently popular.

We played the night clubs in London's West End and if that sounds glamorous – it shouldn't – most of these clubs were upholstered sewers and catered for the dregs of London's night life – the toughest audiences an act could experience – we really earned the standard £15 per week they paid us, but in truth we were young and loved every minute of it.

On one particular engagement we 'doubled'. Doubling meant playing two night clubs in the same evening; at one club The Blue Lagoon we'd begin the cabaret at midnight, then rush to the Panama Club about half a mile away and perform to a different crowd around one a.m.

It was simple for me to put a raincoat over my dinner suit and run the distance to the second date, much more difficult for Tommy who not

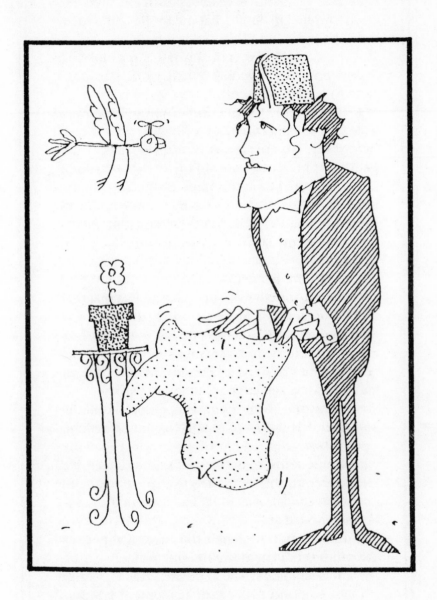

only had to carry two suitcases filled with his tricks but had to 'load', that means he had to prepare the tricks, and this took time.

Tommy would precede me at the first club and follow me at the second. This way he got extra time to get his act ready.

One night, at the second club an irate boss asked if I'd seen Tommy. I knew he had left well before me but there was no sign of him at the Panama Club. The boss told me to do extra and I filled in until I saw the huge shape of Tommy enter and make for the dressing room which was the gents lavatory. When I could see he was ready I wound up my stint and introduced 'The Great Thomas Cooper'.

If you think his tricks went wrong as a top of the bill you should have been at the Panama that night – disaster. I honestly think that was the night he decided to make a living from his tricks misfiring, and the nervous giggle became part of his repertoire. When I asked him afterwards what had made him so late he told me the story:

'I came out of the club, was quickly walking past Garrards the Jewellers in Regent Street and a policeman stepped out of a doorway to ask me what I had in the two cases – I said, "Magic". He said, "Open the cases". I tried to explain that I did a magic act and that all my tricks were in the cases but he insisted.

'Course, when I opened the case all the vases and rings were sparkling under the lights so he became suspicious – he thought I was a burglar who'd just done a job. At that moment another copper strolled up and he happened to be an amateur conjuror, so to prove I was legitimate, he made me perform one of the tricks – so there I was in the middle of Regent Street at half past midnight doing bottle – glass – glass – bottle – bottle – glass...'

He then said, 'Max, I've had a frustrating day, let's get pissed!' So we did.

A middle-aged Australian from the Bush goes on a round-the-world trip alone. Sitting in the first class lounge waiting for his plane, he notices this classy looking young lady with the initials NSW embossed on her brief case; he decides to chat her up.

AUS.:   Excuse me miss, those initials – are you from New South Wales?

GIRL: Oh no – I'm with the Nymphomaniac Society of the World. I'm travelling the world trying to find out which race of men are the greatest lovers.

AUS.:   Is that a fact – have you arrived at any conclusions?

GIRL: Yes – without a doubt, the North American Indians are the greatest.

AUS.:   Is that a fact – who was second?

GIRL: The Jewish race are second – they are marvellous.

AUS.:   Is that a fact?

GIRL: May I ask you your name?

AUS.:   Yes – it's Hiawatha Goldberg.

Zeke was nineteen and lived in Tennessee. One day he shaves himself, changes his shirt from the one he has worn for weeks, adds some aftershave and, spruced up, he wanders on to the verandah where his papa sits in a rocking chair... whittling.

DAD: Where you going, son?

ZEKE: I'm going over to Mary Lou's place, she's now thirteen and I reckon she's ready for courtin'.

DAD: Will you be long, son?

ZEKE: I reckon about three days, I may bring her back as my bride.

Next day Zeke arrives back alone.

DAD: You're back soon Zeke – where's Mary Lou?

ZEKE: I didn't bother, Dad, I found out she was a virgin, so I came back home.

DAD: Yer did right son – if she ain't good enough for her own family, she ain't good enough for ours.

A Cockney who was fed up with marriage, fed up with the mother-in-law and sick of life generally, begins to pack his suitcase.

'Where are you going?' asks his wife.

'I'm going to Australia – my mate told me that women outnumber men three to one – what's more, women there will pay you twenty pounds just to make love to them'.

The wife starts packing her case too.

'Where are *you* going?' asks the Cockney.

His wife says, 'I'm coming with you – I want to see how you're going to live on a pound a week!'

A publisher was curious when he was told there was a salesman working for him who sold more Bibles than any other salesman, in some cases trebling the sales of others. The publisher said he would like to meet him. The salesman was shown into his office.

PUBLISHER: I'm pleased to meet you.

SALESMAN: (A stammerer) I'm p p p pleas – ed to m m m m meet y you sir ....

PUBLISHER: How do you manage to sell so many Bibles?

SALESMAN: W w w well sir, I I I say to the c customer, would you li li like me to r r r read it t t to you?

JACK BENNY

During the 1960s I was invited to appear on The Jack Benny Show in California USA. For most of the time I was there I had dinner with Jack, his wife Mary and several show business friends at his house in Beverly Hills.

After dinner one night, Mary put her coat on to take their poodle for a walk round the block before retiring. Jack and I sat in the lounge armchairs puffing contentedly on two Havana cigars.

On the same block as Jack lived film star James Stewart. He had recently made a movie, *The Glenn Miller Story*. After the filming he liked the idea of the rimless spectacles he used in the film and took to wearing them regularly. Almost every impressionist in America at that time was impersonating James Stewart. It was an easy impression – all one had to do was fish a pair of the rimless glasses out of a pocket and drawl, 'Well ... er ... just a minute ... er ... hold on ...!' thunderous applause, it was so recognisable!

The drawl became a trade mark.

When Mary arrived back at the house with the poodle she said to Jack, 'I just met Jimmy Stewart on the block – he was walking his dog – I said, "How are you Jimmy" and you'd have thought he was doing an impression of himself, he said, (Mary went into an impression),

"Waal...er...look...er...Mary...I...er...er...". She said 'I could stand it no longer. I said "Look Jimmy – it's chilly. I don't want an impersonation, I just want to know how you are!" With that, she told Jack, she walked off.

Jack was flabbergasted, he clapped his hands to his face, as he did on most of his shows, and said in disbelief, 'Oh Mary – you didn't say that to Jimmy!'

The dog began to bark, she looked at her husband and said, '*I told Jimmy top stop doing James Stewart – you* can cut out your impression of Jack Benny and...' (poing to the dog) '...and you can stop your impression of Ethel Merman!'

The payoff to the following joke is better left unsaid.

It is summer and a small boy is playing in the garden whilst his mother and father attend to the tomatoes and weeding. A .butterfly lands on the grass and the small boy stamps on it. His father says, 'You mustn't do that – that's a poor butterfly and you've killed it – for that you get no butter for a week'.

Later on, a honey-bee settles on the grass and the boy steps on that too. 'Don't you realize the bee gives us honey – you've just killed it – for that you get no honey for *two* weeks'.

Later, it's the turn of a cockroach to walk on the grass – without giving it another thought, the mother tramples the cockroach to death. The little boy looks at his mother, then at his father ....

'Answers on a postcard, please!'

JUDY GARLAND

If you ever watched the television series *The Untouchables*, you will remember the narration by the staccato voice delivery of commentator Walter Winchell, probably the most powerful columnist in America during the early 1950s. I was awarded a complimentary line in his column whilst appearing at the Palace, New York, with Judy Garland; from that one line the phone in my hotel room hardly stopped ringing. Top agents MCA wanted me on their books, so did the William Morris Agency. I was wooed by almost the entire show business scene, yet all he said as far as I can remember, was, 'Max Bygraves — funny man from England puts paid to the rumour that Englishmen have no sense of humour – don't miss him....'

Winchell started life in Vaudeville and was a hoofer – how he gave it up to become the most important showbiz newspaper man in the USA I don't know, but he was and remained so for his lifetime. Most people in US showbusiness would have shot their grandmothers for an inch or two in his column and Judy Garland was no exception.

We performed two shows daily at the Palace, New York – a matinée at two-thirty plus an evening show at eight. Most of the theatrical and press people came to the afternoon show, there were no empty seats, every show was a sell out and tickets were as difficult to get as for men's final day at Wimbledon.

The show had been running for several weeks when one Wednesday matinée the buzz went round backstage, 'Winchell's in!' Even the stage hands moved twice as fast.

Wearing the fedora he was famed for, he made his entrance to the stalls, removing the hat only when the lights went down for the overture. By now the entire audience was aware that the great one was in their midst.

With two or more songs still to go, Judy decided to introduce Winchell to the crowd. They cheered and when those in the upper circle loudly complained that they could not see him, he cheerfully left his seat and walked towards the orchestra pit so those above could have a better view. Judy enticed him on to the stage to thunderous applause − he was beaming and loving every moment as the spotlight picked him out.

Judy Garland told him how thrilled she was to have him on stage, they threw compliments at each other, then Winchell surprised Judy by telling her that he had actually worked on this very stage before as a dancer; she was genuinely surprised and asked what sort of dancing he did. Winchell asked the musical director for a stop chorus of 'Bye bye blues', a standard for most dancers. The roof almost fell in as their favourite reporter went into 'a buck and wing'. I stood on the side of the stage watching all this and couldn't believe the standing ovation they gave him for these few simple steps. They cheered him all the way back to his seat. Anything Judy attempted after was an anti-climax − it was a case of 'follow

that!' Next day, there was a glorious review of the Judy Garland Show and everybody was happy.

Two days go by and Winchell turns up again, but this time with a couple of friends – he gets called on again, the applause is even louder, his spot gets longer, he is really stage-struck. The following Monday, he is in again and sends notes backstage to Judy to mention the six friends he has brought, also a couple more questions to ask when she calls him on stage. Slowly the Judy Garland Show is turning into the Walter Winchell Show and Judy isn't too pleased at the way things are going; something has to be done.

Sid Luft, Judy's manager, who later became her husband, hit on the idea of telling Winchell that the Musicians' Union were not allowed to play for any performer who was not a card-carrying Union man. He showed Winchell a letter on MU notepaper that testified to this.

The write-ups on Judy stopped from that moment. Judy was sad but relieved.

Years later, when Winchell had passed away, I met Sid Luft in Bond Street and as we strolled towards Piccadilly, we talked about the Winchell episode. 'It was a good thing the Musicians' Union sent that letter, wasn't it Sid?' He replied, 'It was a good thing my brother-in-law was not only the musical director but the Union representative and had some headed notepaper that we had typed up, otherwise he'd have been on till the day he died!'

The Pope was late for an engagement fifty miles from Rome. He asked the chauffeur to step on the gas; 'I'm already doing 120 in a 60K area, Your Holiness', replied the chauffeur.

The Pope told the driver to move over and let him drive. Sure enough, a police car overtook them and flagged them down; the Pope stopped and the policeman called headquarters on his mobile.

POLICEMAN: I've got a problem: I've just stopped this speeding car and I don't know whether I should give him a ticket – he's pretty important.

HEADQUARTERS: How important? Is he more important than the mayor?

POLICEMAN: Oh yes – he's more important than the Chief of Police – he's even more important than the Queen of England....

HEADQUARTERS: Well, how important is he...?

POLICEMAN: I'll tell you how important he is – the Pope is driving him.

An Irishman goes through a car wash; when he comes out at the other end, the attendant says, 'Two pounds, Paddy'.

'How did you know I was Irish?' asks Paddy.

'We don't get too many coming through here on motor bikes!'

We owe a lot to the Irish – don't forget, in the year 1874 it was an Irishman that invented the very first lavatory seat – and two years later it was an Englishman that cut a hole in it!

A young married man arrives home for lunch one day to find his very flat-chested wife is now the owner of a Jane Russell bust; she looks marvellous. 'What have you got up there – a couple of melons?' She can't contain her excitement. 'No, they're not melons – some gypsies knocked at the door this morning and sold me a mirror – the head gypsy told me that if I made a wish the first time I looked into the mirror it would be granted – I didn't really believe him but when he'd gone, I thought I'd give it a try. I hung the mirror up with eyes closed, then opened them and said, 'Mirror mirror on the door – make my bust a forty-four.' Isn't it marvellous?'

'Yes, it looks really good,' he says admiringly. Breathlessly she asks him to get his own lunch as she must go the shops to purchase a bra. Alone, he looks at the mirror and decides to have a try; he says, 'Mirror mirror on the door – make my ding-a-ling touch the floor!'

And his legs fell off!

When the three vicars arrived at the golden gates, St Peter asked the question he asked all clergymen – 'Did you ever commit adultery?'

If they had been 'having it off', he advised them not to seek entrance but to turn around and go away.

On this particular occasion, he needed advice – he calls Big G. 'Lord – three of the clergy just arrived, I put the usual question, "Did you ever commit adultery?" Two of them turned around and walked back; what shall we do about the deaf one?'

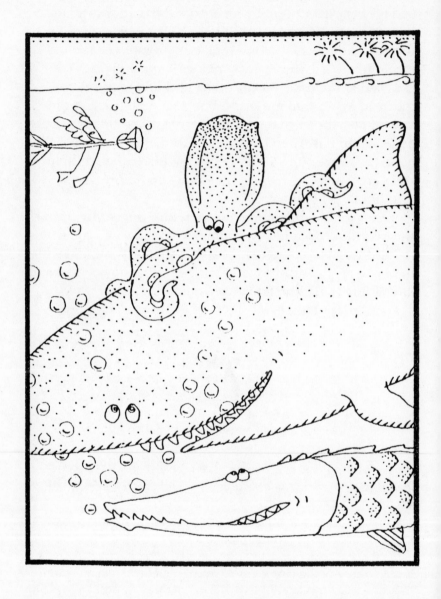

The following joke is among my very favourite stories.

A shark is swimming in the North Sea and comes upon a squid....

SHARK: You don't look well Squid.

SQUID: I'm not well – I feel awful.

SHARK: You know what's wrong with you – you are in the wrong water, it's too cold for you – you shouldn't be in the North Sea, you should be in the warm Mediterranean ....

SQUID: But it's a long way Shark – I haven't got the energy to travel that far.

SHARK: No problem Squid, get on my shoulder, I'll give you a lift.

Three days later, they are in the Med enjoying the warmth of the blue sea. Suddenly, in the distance looms a large barracuda. The shark swims right up to the barracuda, shrugs his shoulder and says:
'Here's that sick squid I owe you.'

PS Don't try telling this to an American, they don't deal in quids and 'sick dollar' doesn't sound the same.

JIMMY TARBUCK

Jimmy Tarbuck is a good comedian – I have seen him 'on form', and there are very few patter comics who can equal his delivery and cheek.

He doesn't always make friends because he usually goes for the laugh regardless of the embarrassment his jokes can sometimes bring, but he doesn't do it to hurt, it's just that he can't resist the sound that is music to any comedian's ears – the sound of laughter.

On a couple of occasions I have had to let him know that I wasn't all that pleased about some gibe he had made about me. I take a lot of stick from impersonators that, at times, get a bit personal and Jimmy in the past has hit below the belt ... but I like him and regard him as a friend – his heart is in the right place and I can assure you he wouldn't hurt you intentionally.

A few years ago, he was in a summer show at Bournemouth. I am a resident of Bournemouth so we met regularly at Parkstone Golf Club for a game. He is a far better golfer than I could ever hope to be, he gave me a generous stroke advantage and we'd play for a couple of golf balls – almost every time he'd win, I had to forfeit two new golf balls.

At the time, Jim had lost his driving licence for speeding and had to use a driver, who also

caddied for him. One day we had played as usual, Jim had won and, as usual, I had to pay with two new golf balls. As I passed his Rolls in the car park, his driver was putting Jim's clubs in the boot. I noticed there was a box of new balls – with a wink to the driver, I took two new balls, unseen by Jim, then walked to the front of the car, gave him his own golf balls with, 'H'y'are Jim – what I owe you'. He took the balls, gave them to his driver to put in the boot of the car, said Cheerio and went off.

The next time we met, I did the same thing and kept it going for half a dozen games – eventually, I took the whole box of twelve balls and, on this particular day, I said, 'Here Jim – you played so well today, I want to give you a box of a dozen balls'. He took them and walked to the boot to put them in with his clubs. A puzzled look came over his face. It was obvious he was missing something. He turned to see the driver and me grinning from ear to ear, he looked at the balls, realised they were his own and with three words summed me up, 'You conniving bastard!'

Jim tells this story quite often. I hope he adds that I did give him a legitimate extra dozen balls as compensation.

A Scotsman arrives in London and gets in a taxi. 'Where can I find the smallest and cheapest brothel in London?'
Without missing a beat, the taxi driver says, 'You're in it!'

A South African walks into the bar of a London hotel; seated alone is a most attractive dark-haired lady. The SA whispers to the barman, 'Ask the lady what she'd like to drink'. The barman says, 'Don't waste your time guv – she's a lesbian'. But the fellow from Johannesburg insists. The barman walks to the end of the bar and asks the lady what she'd like to drink with the SA. He returns and tells him she'll have a gin and tonic. The big oaf pays the barman, then strolls up to the lady and says, 'Cheers! What part of Lesbia are you from?'

I first met Abie in Bournemouth; he owned a small hardware store and was just making a living – not a fortune but he got by.

I often stopped for a chat, because Abie was always cheerful and glad to see you.

I wandered into his store one day and the laughter was gone from his eyes. He explained that Woolworth's were opening a new store right next door to him. I advised him to sell up – he couldn't hope to compete against Woolworth's, but he said he'd try to hang on.

Three months later, he looked worse than last time; the reason was that Marks and Spencer's were going to open on the other side. 'Sell,' I said, but again he said he'd hang on. With Woolworth's one side, Marks and Sparks on the other, he had no chance.

Six months later, I saw him getting out of a Rolls-Royce, tailored suit, silk shirt, diamond cufflinks. 'Did you sell, Abie?' I asked. 'No, I just changed the name over the door', he smiled. 'What to?'

He smiled again, 'Main Entrance!'

We were in Calgary, Canada, watching the rodeo. The bronco busting was getting cheers as the riders were unseated by the energy of the animals. Suddenly, over the public address system came an announcement: 'Anybody in the crowd that can ride the bronco and stay seated for ten seconds will be paid one hundred dollars'. Several volunteers were unseated in less than five seconds. Suddenly, a slightly built bloke in his fifties stands up and calls, 'I'll have a go!' His wife said, 'Sit down Ernie – don't make a fool of yourself'. But he persists, the crowd urges him on and to everybody's surprise, he rides the wild bronco to a standstill; the crowd cheered and clapped. He collects the hundred dollars – comes back to his seat handing the money to his wife, who looks at him in unbelieving admiration. 'Gee Ernie, I didn't know you could ride – where did you learn to hang on like that?'

Ernie nodded his head modestly and said, 'Well Edna, remember when you had whooping cough...?'

An elderly Irish priest had never been outside Dublin in his lifetime and he astounded Mother Superior when he told her that he was gong for a long weekend to London. She urges him to be careful and, sure enough, as he walks through the Soho district, the ladies of the evening accost him.

'Want a quickie for five pounds?' He ignores them but they still implore, 'Come on vicar – five pounds for a quickie!'

When the priest arrives back in Dublin, he phones Mother Superior. 'Mother – I wonder if you could tell me, what is a "quickie"?'

'Five pounds – same as London!' she says.

A large Scottish sailor was berating a shop assistant at a souvenir shop in Hong Kong.

SAILOR: I just paid twenty cents for this fan, I fluttered it and it broke.

ASSISTANT: Scusee, please?

SAILOR: Never mind the scusee please – twenty cents I paid for the fan, now it's all broke....

ASSISTANT: Scusee sir, when only pay twenty cents for fan don't flutter – hold fan still, shakee head!

A couple, both aged sixty and living in Sydney. He surprises her one evening by saying, 'Look Lil, I'm sixty years old – same as you – and I've decided to retire – I've made quite a bit of money and before I settle down I'd like to have a last fling'.

He then tells her he'd like to take a two-week holiday by the sea at Surfer's Paradise alone – then he will find a twenty-year-old Sheila and live it up.

His wife is not too happy with the idea but thinks it might get it out of his system if she doesn't object. Three days go by and he phones her from Surfer's.

'How are you doing?' she asks.

'I'm having the time of my life Lil – I've found a twenty-year-old Sheila, we go out dancing – go to restaurants – she comes back to the hotel, we have drinks – what are you doing Lil?'

She says, 'I went round to a few pubs in Sydney and found myself a twenty-year-old fella – a youngie – so handsome – and I wanna tell you, 20 goes into 60 more times than 60 goes into 20!'

MR JONES

I never really thought much about bank managers. At one time, I did think they were the nice, placid fellows we saw on television commercials who said, 'How can we help?' But since I stood guarantor for a relative whose business went down the gurgler, I am not of the same opinion. If you are solvent and they can use your money to add a few extra per cent by re-lending it, you remain 'a valued customer', their profits remain in the high millions. My relative needed a little more time, the recent recession had clobbered some hardworking people who were trying to survive, but alas, the nasty letters began to arrive from the bank. This came as a big shock: I have never had a loan from a bank or anybody else in forty years. My first house had a £3000 mortgage but I paid that up quickly. The letters that threatened litigation got tougher and more worrying, so I had to pay for peace of mind. I'd guaranteed £150,000, not a lot by Alan Bond, or Maxwell, standards but enough to make a vow never to lend again – ever. There was a lot of hard work attached to earning that amount.

The day I walked out of the bank that wouldn't listen, I went to my car parked on a meter outside the bank. Terror as I felt for the keys. Lost? No, I could see them hanging from the steering wheel in the car; the little Nissan was locked solidly all round. I stood helpless trying to figure a way to get into my wife's new car without damaging it.

How do car thieves do it?

The bank was now closed. I thought I'd try a friendly dry cleaner's next door and ask to use their phone. I knew we had a spare set of keys at home, perhaps my wife could put them in a cab – it would take a good forty-five minutes but that was the only alternative. She was out, the phone rang off the wall but no reply.

Just then, the bank manager I had tried to reason with came out and locked the doors of the High Street Bank. He noticed dejected me.

'Are you still here Mr Bygraves?' he asked. I muttered something about the keys being locked in the car. 'No worries, sir – I'll fix it', he smiled.

He went into the dry cleaner's and re-appeared with a thin wire coat hanger. Humming *Tulips from Amsterdam*, he pushed the wire through the side of the door, brought it down to the knob that locked the door, lifted it and presto! opened the door.

'Where did you learn to do that, Mr Jones?' I enquired.

'A friend of mind taught me a few years ago'.

'Well, give him my thanks and if we ever meet up, I'll buy him a drink'.

'I'll do that ...' said Jonesy, '... he gets out in another three years'.

The moral of this story ... if it ever happens to you – and it seems to happen to all car owners at some time – don't call a car thief – call a bank manager.

TED RAY

Ted Ray was a fine comedian and a practical joker, right up to the end of his life. He had appeared in one of my television shows and was a big hit – we became firm friends.

I went to visit him at the Middlesex Hospital – he was in a bad way, the car accident he was involved with left him a broken leg, a fractured arm and they were grafting skin to various parts of his anatomy.

I took him smoked salmon, champagne, a cake and lots of tit bits. In no time we had the sister and nurses in for a small party. After a couple of hours Ted looked exhausted and the sister tipped me off that it was time for Ted to rest. They all left and I was the last to say farewell, but like all comedians from the old school, they've learned 'always leave on a laugh – that way they remember you next time you make an entrance'. Ted Ray had been reared in that school.

Through glazed eyes, Ted thanked me for coming and pulled himself together to tell me a final story: 'A few nights ago I needed a bed pan. It had gone midnight and I was desperate – I rang and rang the bell but no nurse came so I attempted to do something about it. I lifted the bed covers off me; slid slowly to the end of the bed and managed to get to the pot with the plant in. I took the plant out, managed to place the pot on the floor, undid my pyjamas and managed to sit on it. Just as I did the door opened; a light went on and there was Eamonn Andrews who said, 'Ted Ray – tonight This is your Life!'

Shortly after this, Ted passed on.

After a jewel robbery at a large London store, a detective
from the CID was taking statements from witnesses. One
Cockney observer gave the following account.

'It was Sunday morning and the street was very quiet – I
was sitting up in my flat right across the road there. I
noticed a large pantechnicon draw up and park outside the

store – two men got out – opened the back doors of the van and out stepped an *elephant*!

'The elephant was led to the window of the jewellery store and rammed his head against the plate glass which shattered.

'The two men helped themselves to most of the jewels in the window – put the elephant back in the van and drove off.

The detective taking the statement asked if it was an Indian elephant or an African elephant.

'What's the difference?'

'The Indian elephant has ears close to its head – the African elephant has the wide floppy ears' explained the CID man.

'I couldn't help you there – it had a stocking over its head!'

ROSE

'Anything for a dare' that's what they called Rose
Who decided to swim in the sea with no clothes
With not a stitch on, she tripped over the sands
And to cover her bosom she used both her hands

A little boy fishing, looked up in surprise
And couldn't believe what he saw with his eyes
'If you're drowning those puppies,' he shouted to Rose
'...can I have the one with the little pink nose?'

ERIC SYKES

We have been pals for more than 40 years. If he or I needed a friend I think we would call on each other first. Eric is a very fine script writer and a very funny man. He first learned of this latent comedy when we were both signed for the BBC show *Educating Archie*, a show that won many awards. Apart from Eric and myself the show unearthed a wealth of talent, Tony Hancock, Julie Andrews, Beryl Reid, Hattie Jacques and quite a few more.

When we were first given the scripts, usually on Sunday morning to be performed 'live' Sunday evening, we'd read our parts in flat early morning voices. It was the inflection of the delivery that brought Eric's scripts to life. It was how Hancock's 'Flippin' Kids' was born and how I made a national catch phrase of 'A good idea son!'

It was because of this early morning reading Eric decided to read his own comedy lines. It was usually half an hour of hilarity as he played each part himself; from this he managed to give us laughs that were unseen on a first reading, now we all knew how to attack the script.

From this his confidence grew until the series came to an end. He then entered the film world and his silent movies like *The Plank* and others plus the long-running television series with Hattie Jacques endeared him to audiences worldwide.

We became keen golfers together and have become quite competent players, but in the early

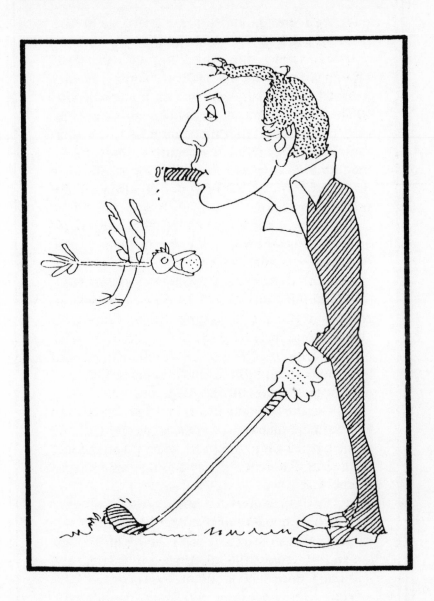

days, we were like most others that take up the game – hackers!

It was during these 'hacking' days that Eric bought a house for his growing family; he had married a lovely lady who was his nurse when he suffered ear trouble and was hospitalized in London. Edith nursed him then and has looked after him since. They lived in a beautiful home, backing on to St Georges Hill at Weybridge. She also provided them with four super children – I am godfather to one.

About the time I am talking about, the mid-1950s, it was reported that I was the highest paid performer in Great Britain.

I was almost resident comedian at the London Palladium, on radio every week, best selling records, television, my name was on billboards all over London. (I have to tell you this because it has a bearing on the story.) I thought it would have been impossible to have been British and not know the name of Max Bygraves.

Back to the hacking. It was Eric's greatest wish to become a member of St Georges Hill GC; his home backed on to the third hole, it would have been so convenient and he had made an application to join.

On this particular day we were out on the course, having paid our fees and got permission to play. As we searched for a lost ball on the fourth hole, two golf balls landed quite near us without a 'Fore!', 'Lookout' or 'Kiss my foot!'

Soon after, two irate red-faced 'gentlemen', and I use the word loosely, humphed their way past bristling with anger; later on many more golfers 'came through', Eric and I thought that was all part of golf etiquette, we went on looking for our balls. We were that inexperienced.

A couple of days later Eric received a letter from the club secretary. I can't remember it word for word but in essence it read:

> Dear Mr Sykes
> You interrupted a competition on this course today – no courtesy was extended to the competitors and your manners leave a lot to be desired.
> We understand you are desirous of becoming a member of this club; if this is the behaviour we are to expect we beg you not to bother. This applies to your partner MAX HARGREAVES.
> Yours etc

All this happened more than thirty-five years ago – Eric who *still* lives nearby and *still* enjoys golf is *still* not a member.

A Jewish immigrant with his two small sons arrives at Heathrow from Israel.

He questions a taxi driver: 'How much to take me to Golders Green?' The taxi driver says, 'I'll do it for twenty pounds'. The Jewish arrival considers, then asks, 'How much for the little boys?'

'Don't worry about the lads, I take them for nothing'.

The Jew considers again. 'Well look – take the boys and I'll walk'.

Two Jewish gentlemen in the clothes business are having a bad time. One of them out 'on the road' calls his partner. 'How are things?'

'How are things? I'll tell you how things are. I can't keep up with the orders – Marks and Spencer's been on the phone with orders – two thousand skirts immediately; British Home Stores want seven thousand ladies' blouses; God knows how we're going to supply Littlewood's....'

The man out on the road says, 'OK Hymie – I'll call back when there's nobody there!'

The old gentleman shuffles up to the nurse at the reception of the hospital and asks to be directed to the sperm bank; he tells them he would like to be a donor.

He arrives at the sperm bank and although the doctor is doubtful she gives the old man a jar and asks him to call the nurse when he has made his donation.

Half an hour later when there is no sign of the octogenarian, the nurse takes a peep behind the screen and finds him perspiring, red-faced and out of breath.

'Are you having trouble?' she asks.

'Yes – I tried ten minutes with the right hand – ten minutes with the left hand – I still can't get the lid off the jar!'

Three men stranded on a desert island were from England, Ireland and Australia – they had been there so long they were utterly fed up with each other.

One sunny morning a bottle with a cork in was washed up on the sand; the Englishman picked it up and pulled the cork out – suddenly whoosh! a Genie appeared from out of the bottle.

'Thank you Master,' he bellowed. 'I have been prisoner in that perishing bottle for more than a thousand years. For releasing me you and your friends can have any one wish you choose; but one wish only!'

The Englishman, astounded by this but not wishing to lose such a wonderful opportunity said, 'If I could have one wish it would be to leave this cursed island and be in my club in Piccadilly having a Scotch and soda with old friends.'

Suddenly there is another whoosh and the Englishman has vanished, his wish fulfilled.

The Australian seeing this says, 'Well Genie, if you'd like to do a cobber a real favour, I'd like to be back in Sydney cuddling up to my favourite Sheila with a crate of Four X between us!'

Whoosh! He is on his way down under. The Genie turns to Paddy and says, 'You Sir – what is your one wish?'

The Irishman thinks for a moment – looks around and says, 'It's lonely here without the other two – I wish they were back again!'

DANNY LA RUE

You would travel a long journey to find a more generous person than Danny La Rue — his gifts and kindness to people he likes are legendary. He has survived in a crowded profession on sheer talent, as a female impersonator he has no equal and although the years are passing many of us by he still manages to attract audiences at home and abroad and leave 'em laughing.

If anybody was to ask me what his faults were I could only think of one — he loves to rabbit — he really could talk the hind leg off the proverbial donkey. When Danny gets a touch of the verbals it's best to shut up and listen or say, 'We must get home 'cos of the babysitter!' Let me tell you a Danny La Rue story.

My wife Blossom and I went to see his show at the Regent Theatre in Sydney, Australia. The show was great; afterwards we were invited backstage to Danny's dressing room and we were told by Jack Hanson his road manager that Danny was on the other side of the stage talking to some members of the Sydney Ballet Corps, he would not be long. Jack gave us a glass of champagne and we waited....

We were both hungry having had no food from breakfast time and Sydney, like most cities, seems to close down food-wise after eleven p.m. so we waited....

Blossom is glancing at her watch every two minutes. Then after almost twenty minutes waiting, she came out with a classic line that Danny dines out on.... 'We didn't have to wait this long for the real Queen!'

A man was bragging in a pub one day
About a big dog that he owns
This dog for breakfast eats four pounds of meat
And twenty-six pounds of bones

'I've got a dog' said a little old man
'A little old dog we call Willim
And I'll bet if mine had a fight with yours
I'll bet ten quid mine'd kill him'.

So the two dogs met the very next day
And in no time the big dog was dead
'Cos the little old man's dog opened his mouth
And bit off the big one's head.

The little old man patted his dog
And said to the crowd with a smile
'Before this dog had a head transplant
This dog was a crocodile!'

The owner of a racehorse at Epsom has quick look around, then puts his hand in his pocket and feeds the horse a tit bit.

The Clerk of the Course comes over to the owner and asks what was it he put in the horse's mouth. 'Sugar', says the owner, 'here, taste it'. The owner has some, then dips his hand into his pocket again and produces a piece for the Clerk to taste; the Clerk swallows it, seems satisfied and off he goes.

Now the owner whispers to his jockey, 'I'll tell you how to run this race – first five furlongs hold him back – on the last three furlongs give him his head and let him go. If anybody passes you don't worry – it will be me and the Clerk of the Course!'

ANTHONY AND THE WALLET

Most families have a gathering, at weddings, funerals, Christmas etc where the favourite family story is trotted out time and time again. Our family is no exception; one of the yarns they enjoy most is the tale of Anthony and the Wallet. It happened many moons ago when I took Blossom and the children for two weeks' holiday at a luxury hotel in Jersey. Anthony, my son, was about seven or eight at the time.

I would crack gags about him 'training to be a miser', I would tell of a tramp that knocked at our street door; Anthony answered the knock, the tramp said, 'Any old clothes?' Anthony said, 'Yes, please!' We arrived on the Saturday, I gave the three children £5 each and told them that was their holiday spending money. The two girls spent half of it over the weekend but Anthony invested sixpence in a plastic wallet. The pound notes, the ten shilling note and the silver was compartmented in the wallet which he kept on him at all times. He is one of the most generous people you could wish to meet nowadays but in those days he was tighter than a duck's arse – and that's watertight.

That night as we were going to bed I heard this shrill cry come from the children's bedroom. I rushed in the room to find Anthony sobbing and our babysitter Phyllis laughing uncontrollably. It took quite a while to get the story out of her.

This is what happened. Anthony decided that if burglars came in the night they wouldn't find his wallet if he hid it under the mattress of his bed. After about five minutes he reckoned that was the first place they would look so he got out of bed and moved the wallet from the mattress and placed it underneath the carpet.

After another five minutes or so, he decided that that hiding place was not good enough so he got out of bed again and found another hiding place; this was in a cupboard next to his bed that contained a china chamber. He dropped the wallet in the pot and got back in bed.

After a short while he decided again to find a safer place so he proceeded to take the wallet out, only to discover that the pot had been used by the previous guest and had not been emptied – no wonder Phyllis was collapsing with laughter every time she thought of the situation. She laughed even more when I gallantly retrieved the wallet, took it into the bathroom to wash the muck off, then put the notes on the radiator to dry.

The last time I told that story was to friends and relations at my property in Australia last Christmas. I had flown out the entire family (twelve) for an Oz Xmas and once more Anthony had to listen to the tale of the wallet.

Anthony, who never misses a chance to make a pun, murmured for my ears only, 'I remember it well – I was really *pissed* off!'

These two punks, Spottie and Acne, meet.

'Wow!' says Spottie, 'I like your hair – magic – Wow! It looks great! Does it take long to get it like that?'

'Yes,' says Acne. 'If I'm going somewhere special it can take me four hours to get it looking like this!'

'Well it's worth it – that's real class. 'Ere Spottie – what would you do if a bird crapped in your hair?'

'I don't think I'd go out with her again!' says Acne.

There are two take-away restaurants in Soho – one a Greek, the other Chinese. The Greek proprietor annoys the Chinese owner by running in each day shouting, 'Any flied lice today?' Every day it's the same,'Any flied lice?'

The Chinese manager gets so fed up with the Greek, he decides to take a crash course in English – he hires a tutor – buys Linguaphone and several different books on English. Sure enough, three months later the Greek pokes his head in to ask, 'Any flied lice?'

The Chinese owner, in impeccable English, suddenly says 'Excuse me old chap – I think what you are trying to say is 'Any *fried rice*?' It is pronounced *fried rice* you Gleek Plick!'

A broad Irishman in a London pub shouts to the piano player, 'Give us a jazz chord'. The pianist to oblige does a few bars à la George Shearing.

'Naw – a jazz chord!' He tried to oblige with a few bars of Oscar Peterson. 'Can't you play a jazz chord'. The fed up pianist shouts back, 'I've just played a bloody jazz chord!' The Irishman, filled with Guinness, shouts 'Naw – Stevie Wonder's A jazz chord to say I love you – a jazz chord to say I care ....'

SEAN CONNERY

I have often said that if you play a man three rounds of golf you'll find out the man's true nature, whether he's polite, a cheat, single-minded, good fun; almost every quality comes to the surface and after eighteen holes you will know your partner pretty well.

I have played several times with Sean, seen his eyes blaze at a bad shot, seen him get short-tempered at being held up by a slow game ahead and listened to him wax lyrical about his childhood days in Edinburgh. He's a good bloke.

Today he is a fine amateur golfer but this story took place when he was like most of us beginners — bloody awful!

It was at Coombe Hill GC just outside London, Eric Sykes and I took on Sean and actor Stanley Baker, later knighted. We beat them hands down. Afterwards in the club house Sean came up and placed £60 on the counter with, 'Here y'are Max — you'll find that correct'. I asked Sean what the money was for; he explained we had a £20 bet on the first nine holes, £20 on the second and £20 on the game, ... 'that's £60' he smiled.

I was puzzled by this — I had never played for this amount — the most I ever wagered was a couple of quid on a game. As Sean walked away Eric Sykes entered. I told him that Sean had just paid me £60. A couple of hundred quid by today's standard.

Eric told me that Stanley Baker had just paid

him the same amount. 'Did you make the bet?' I asked Eric. He confessed that Sean had mumbled something in his Scottish accent and Eric, whose hearing is defective, just nodded his head, so Sean assumed we had a bet on.

As Eric and I drank our drinks our eyes met and we began to laugh – laugh hysterically because we were both thinking the same thing –'What a fight there would have been if we'd *lost*!'

'That's my husband at the back door!' gasps an unfaithful wife. 'Go out the front door,' she urges.

'I haven't got a stitch on', the lover protests.

'He'll kill you, if he discovers you,' she says pushing him out on to the street. At that moment, a bunch of joggers go by, lover boy joins them....

JOGGER: You're new on this run, aren't you?

LOVER BOY: Yes – first time.

JOGGER: Thought I hadn't seen you before – do you know you're wearing a condom?

LOVER BOY: Er – yes, it was raining when I came out!

An unfaithful wife tells her lover to hide in the wardrobe when her husband comes home unexpectedly. As he stands in the wardrobe hardly daring to breathe, a small boy's voice whispers, "Dark in here, ain't it?'

'Who are you?' asks Lover Boy.

'That's my mummy out there putting her clothes on and that's my daddy who's just arrived home – shall I tell him you're in here?'

'No don't do that son – here – here's a little present for you'. He gives the voice all the money he has – abut £15. 'Just be quiet'.

Next morning at the breakfast table, the little boy gets all the money LB has given him and begins to count it....

DAD: Where did you get so much money, son?

BOY: A man gave it to me.

DAD: A man? Who was the man?

BOY: I couldn't tell you Dad – it was too dark.

The father decides the boy is telling lies – he tells him he likes to bring him up as a good Catholic and that he must not tell him lies like this again. As a lesson he walks him to the church and pushes him into the confessional box.

When the boy gets in the confessional (his first time) he whispers, 'Dark in here – ain't it?'

The priest groans, 'Oh God – it's not you again'.

A highly sexed beauty is enjoying a cruise in the Pacific —
the boat pulls into a remote desert island, she decides to
swim ashore and is confronted by a naked castaway who
speaks the same language as herself; she asks...

GIRL: How long have you been here?

CASTAWAY: I've lost count, we were shipwrecked when I
               was a small boy many years ago and I've
               been here ever since....

GIRL: How do you exist?

CASTAWAY: I eat fruit from the trees, I catch fish and most
               of the day I dig for clams....

GIRL: (Eyeing his great physique) What do you do
               for sex?

CASTAWAY: Sex – what's sex?

GIRL: (She draws him close and demonstrates until
               he is exhausted). That's sex – did you like it?

CASTAWAY: No, I did not.

GIRL: Why not?

CASTAWAY: Look what you've done to my clam digger!

GEORGE BURNS

I knew George Burns when he was a much younger man – he was only seventy-six.

Today, he is heading for his hundredth year. He had flown over from California to London for a one-off appearance on my Thames Television show. We have kept in touch.

I'll never forget our first meeting. It was at the Dorchester Hotel, he had given me his room and floor number. I went straight up and knocked at the door and a small frail bald-headed man answered dressed in a burgundy silk dressing gown.

'Is Mr George Burns here?' I asked.

'Just a minute,' said the little old man and went back into the same room.

The same little old man emerged about twenty seconds later; this time he wore a silver toupé, thick glasses and smoked a nine-inch cigar.

'What can I do for you?' asked George Burns. The transformation was astounding – I just stood there laughing.

'What are you laughing at – did you never meet a leprechaun?'

That was exactly what he looked like; so many people must have said so, he decided to get in first. We became friends from that day on. He told me so many stories, it was hard to sort out the truth from the fantasy but there was never a silent minute with George, he filled in every moment.

He would talk of Al Jolson '... not a great guy as a friend but a superb entertainer, "unashamed schmaltz".' He'd tell of Fanny Brice, Sophie Tucker, Sam Goldwyn, Ronald Colman and many many more, all first hand and for somebody like myself, content just to sit and listen – it went on for more than two weeks – at rehearsal – at dinner – in the limousine, what's more, he never repeated himself.

Many of his stories had macabre pay-offs, like the following. Think of George telling it between puffs of his Havana corona ....

'You think of fans that adored people like Sinatra and Johnny Ray? The equivalent in our day was George M Cohan, the great American songwriter and entertainer – he would give five shows a day and the crowd for the next show would be queued round the block waiting to get in.

'Between shows, Mr Cohan and the supporting cast would take refreshment in the Green Room, then get ready for the next performance. It was a great honour to be on the same bill as George M Cohan; he played all the best dates; the auditorium was always a sell out and your date book was filled for many months.

'At the beginning of a tour that opened in Philadelphia, two hoofers (male dancers) joined the show; they had not been in the business long and were wide-eyed at being on the very same programme as the great George M Cohan.

'One afternoon, between shows in the Green Room, one of the dancers plucked up courage to talk to George M who was in deep thought at the end of the bar. He said, "Mr Cohan this is the greatest thrill of our lives, we are new to show business and to be an opening act on the George M Cohan tour is beyond belief – it would give us so much pleasure if we could buy you a drink".

'George M then explained that he had just received some bad news: he had just lost his mother and would prefer to be alone, to which the youngest dancer replied, "We know how you feel: two weeks ago – we lost our suitcases".'

The driver of a vehicle involved in a smash was not wearing a seat belt and as he shot through the windscreen both ears were severed.

An hour later, at the hospital, the surgeon decided to graft another pair of ears on the patient. Unfortunately, there were no human ears left in the spare organs bank – only pigs' ears.

The family was consulted and permission for the pigs' ears to be grafted on was given. The surgeon did a fine job and the family were allowed a visit.

The visiting wife decided to bring a Walkman complete with headphones to see if her husband's hearing was affected.

He tried them on and listened with the new pigs' ears.

'Are they alright?' enquired the wife.

'Not too bad, but there's a bit of crackling in the left ear!'

Two Irish labourers passing a job centre – one said 'Look, tree fellers wanted'. The other one said, 'What a pity there's only two of us!'

A fellow from Kerry saw a notice outside a police station. 'Man Wanted For Murder'. He went in and applied for the job!

A quartet of golfing pals play every Sunday morning and the wives of these players finally rebel. 'Look – you're at work all week – the kids never see you 'cos you' get home too late and Sundays you spend on the golf course – it has got to stop!!' So they stop.

Three months pass and one of them phones the other

three and says, 'We haven't had a game in twelve weeks, surely the wives can't complain if we have a round next Sunday'. They meet on the first tee the following Sabbath and the conversation goes like this:

1ST GOLFER: This is the most expensive game of golf I've ever played – before I came here today, I had to promise to buy the wife a new fur coat....

2ND GOLFER: You should talk – my wife wants a cruise round the Mediterranean with her mother. I had to foot the bill for that.

3RD GOLFER: My wife demanded a new bedroom suite – set me back two grand.

4TH GOLFER: It didn't cost me a penny.

1, 2 & 3: How come – what did you do? Tell us.

4TH GOLFER: I was lying in bed this morning, I turned to the wife and said, 'Golf course or intercourse?' She said, 'Don't forget your sweater!'

A startled fellow goes into the doctor's office and says, 'I just saw a nun leave here, she looked frightened to death'.

The doctor says, 'I was responsible, I told her she was pregnant'.

The fellow gulps, 'Isn't that unusual?' The doctor said 'She wasn't really – but it cured her hiccups!'

BENNY HILL

If you were to ask me who was the most famous comedian in the world, I would have to say Benny Hill. The last time we were together, he told me that his Thames Television shows were being shown in twenty-eight countries, probably more now, they show them and re-run them for ages.

Possibly also the richest funny man around, his fame was unbelievable. Once on a QEII cruise, we were just leaving Rio de Janeiro, when a young honeymoon couple, hearing my English voice, asked if I had ever heard of Benny Hill and I boastfully told them I *knew* him. They gazed at me as if I was the Messiah – they followed me around the ship for almost a week. On the same trip we made stop at Tristan de Cunha in the South Atlantic, population 187, all Spanish speaking. A woman who had been evacuated to England when the volcano was threatening to erupt passed me a note to see if it was possible to get a signed picture of Benny when I got back to the UK. I gave him the note on my return and he was more surprised than I was, that somebody so remote should know of his work.

As I said, he was fabulously wealthy but didn't bother too much with money – his greatest stimulant came from his work and to make a gag or funny routine come to life was really all he cared about. The press tried on several occasions to make copy from his spartan way of life, but I don't think Benny even bothered to buy a newspaper, I don't think he knew or cared about the monetary rewards.

This story isn't too much about Benny, it concerns a friend of mine named Johnny Kelly.

Johnny is now retired and lives in Bognor down in Sussex. At one time, he owned the Hillingdon Social Club just a few miles from central London. This was in the late forties, just after the war and people generally were in the mood to be entertained. Johnny kept me going with regular bookings at the club where I always did extremely well with the audience. £3 a show.

There was one particular day in late summer I couldn't make a date because of a full week's engagement in Jersey. I wrote to Johnny to say how sorry I was but recommended a pal I had met who was vacant and would appear for £2.50 (two pounds ten shillings in those days). I told him his name was Benny Hill and I said in the letter '...I promise he won't let you down'.

Johnny still carries the note around – it's held together by/sellotape but he will produce it any time the occasion demands.

Not too long ago, I was appearing in Bognor and Johnny came to say hello. Sure enough, the note came out – Johnny gazed at it in disbelief – shook his balding head and murmured, 'Imagine – Benny Hill for fifty bob!'

'Did you ever book him?' I asked.

'No fear – he was too bloody expensive!'

An Irish girl stopped the lovemaking for a minute, then jumped out of bed. Pointing at her bewildered bedmate she asked, 'You haven't got Aids have you?'

'Of course I haven't got Aids,' said Seamus.

Getting back in bed she said, 'Good – 'cos I couldn't go through that again!'

Two pals meet and greet each other.

JOE: How's things?

HARRY: Terrible. I get migraine so badly.

JOE: I suffered with that – I'll tell you how I cured it – I went home one afternoon – the wife took her blouse off – I put my head in her bosom and for five minutes she stroked the back of my neck, then for another five minutes we kissed passionately – I have never had migraine since ....

HARRY: I must try that.

JOE: You should.

Four weeks later they meet again.

JOE: Hello Harry – how's the migraine?

HARRY: I'm cured! I did exactly what you said – I went home – the wife took her blouse off – I put my head in her bosom – she stroked the back of my neck for five minutes – we kissed for five minutes and now I feel great – and Joe, you've got a beautiful home!

FRANKIE HOWERD

We first met at the BBC − two young men recently demobbed, Frank from the Army, myself from the RAF. We were about the same age − same weight and height and both had the same dreams of making our way in show business. On this particular day, we were auditioning for a producer named Joy Russell-Smith who was on the look out for new talent to be included in a radio show called *Variety Band Box*.

'I was hopeless', said this gangling youth who was very soon to become one of the great post-war comics ... 'all I could think of was ooh aah oh ooh − I couldn't remember a line − I fluffed everything'.

He really was nervous and I couldn't help thinking at the time that if I ever got in that state, I'd find some other job.

Little did he know that those oohs and aahs were to impress the BBC producers so much that in another year Frank was to be a household name.

It was one of those auditions where somebody said, 'Thanks for coming − leave your name and address and we'll contact you'. You left your name and address but never expected to hear another word.

We didn't hear anything for almost three months. In the meantime we both got booked for

a touring revue, *For the Fun of it*, produced by bandleader Jack Payne, opening in Sheffield 29 July 1946. I shared a dressing room and digs with Frank up and down the British Isles for the next nine months and got to know him very well – we remained friends for the rest of his life, which at the time of writing was yesterday.

Frank had his ups and downs but always came back, was always able to capture a new breed of audience when he had exhausted another. He became bigger than ever with the part of the Roman slave in television's *Up Pompeii*. He also fancied himself as a clairvoyant, always wanting to read hands – pretty accurate too.

I have never been one for fortune telling but Frank would insist on giving a reading at least once a week – 'One day, you will be a millionaire', he prophesied. You can imagine my reaction – living in digs that cost £2.50 a week; one suit and wondering what would happen when the tour was over; no trade; a wife and baby to support; the only help we had was from my wife's sister who let us have a room at her house for five shillings a week and here's this amateur fortune teller telling me, 'One day you'll be a millionaire'. All I could say was, 'Frank, I think you've got your wires crossed'.

It was the middle of last year I heard he had been poorly; I called him on the phone and asked if he'd like to have lunch, he said he would and I chose one of the best restaurants in London, just the two of us. We talked mostly nostalgia and I asked if he still read hands, he said he did, he took my hand and gazed at my palm for a long time. 'Didn't I tell you that one day you'd be a millionaire?' I nodded. 'Didn't it come true?' I nodded again, he gave me my hand back and said, 'Well – in that case – pay the bill'. He made a hasty exit and that was the last time I saw dear Frank alive.

A friend of mine painted his bathroom
When his wife rushed in from the street
She dashed past him to the toilet
And he shouted, 'Don't sit on the seat!'

But his wife didn't hear – she only just made it
And she sat there thinking 'What luck'
But as she tried to rise – tears came to her eyes
And she shouted out, 'Help me – I'm stuck!'

My friend pushed and pulled for a full half an hour
Then an idea came into his head
He undid the bolts and with the seat still stuck on
He lifted her on to the bed

Then he rang for the doctor and when he arrived
He said, 'Doctor I'm so glad you've come'
Then he showed him his wife on all fours on the bed
And the doctor just sucked his thumb

'Oh doctor – oh doctor – what can I do?
It was my fault, I take all the blame'
The kind doctor said, 'It's a very nice picture
But I'm not sure that I like the frame!'

A married woman is having an affair when her husband
arrives home unexpectedly.

'Quick,' she says, 'hide in the bathroom'. He does and the
husband who is bursting for a pee dashes past his wife and
finds his wife's lover naked, standing in the middle of the

bathroom clapping his hands. 'What are you doing?' asks the husband.

'Oh, I'm from Rentokil (Clap!) I've been sent (Clap!) ... to get rid of the moths! (Clap!)

'Get rid of the moths?' says the husband – 'but you haven't got a stitch on!'

'I know...,' says the lover, '...little buggers aren't they!'

A new window cleaner at the maternity hospital has cleaned the outside of the windows and now wants to shine the insides but can't get the window open. He knocks on the window and shouts to the woman in the nearest bed, 'How can I get in there?' Half a dozen new mothers all shout together, 'Get stuffed – same as we did!'

A fellow gets in a taxi, gives an address and sits back. He almost jumps out of his skin as the driver goes right through a red light. 'Hey driver, that was a red light you went through!'

The driver smilingly shouts back, 'Don't worry, my brother goes through the red lights all the time'.

The passenger wipes a bead of sweat from his brow. 'Never mind your brother – watch the road'.

They come to another set of lights, the driver does the same crazy thing, straight through a steady red.

The passenger, really frightened, shouts 'For God's sake be careful, that light was at red!'

Unperturbed, the driver again shouts, 'Don't worry, my brother goes through red lights all the time!'

They come to a light at green and the driver slams his brakes on.

'What are you doing – the light's at green, you can go!'

The driver says, 'No fear – my brother might be coming across!'

BILL SHANKLAND

If ever I hear a story of the worm turning or somebody receives a come uppance, I get a glow. I guess most people do, so you can imagine how happy I was to hear this yarn from an old pal of mine, Bill Shankland, whose name may be familiar to some.

He was a professional golfer of some repute in the old days and even though he is in his eighties, he *still* drives a ball from the tee that seems to go to outer space. He *still* has a physique that reminds you of the Berlin wall that was – I would *still* hate to get a clout from those massive hands.

Tony Jacklin was once an assistant to him and speaks of Bill with great affection. In fact I have yet to meet anybody who has met Bill that doesn't have a great deal of affection for 'Maestro', as he is known at our club in Bournemouth.

Bill is now a senior citizen and during the week can be seen walking to the small post office in Canford Cliffs to collect his and his ailing wife's pension. Only a short while ago, after drawing the allowance, he was 'jumped' by a mugger who must have thought Bill would have been a pushover. What a mistake! Bill was also a rugby player of fame in his native New South Wales and his old skills could never have left him. As he ducked the mugger's jump, Bill threw him, the footpad was surprised but must have thought he had timed it badly, he came at Bill full frontal and eighty-one-year-old Bill gave him a fourpenny one right on the point of the chin. The incredible part of this true story is that as the dazed mugger lay on the ground nursing his fractured jaw, he pointed at Bill and cried to the small crowd that had gathered, 'I want you to witness what this man did to me – cos I'm suing him for assault!'

Two dyslexic skiers were discussing how to ski down a mountain in Switzerland. They studied the map in the hostel.

1ST SKIER: I think we should start from the west side of the mountain, then come zag-zig – zag-zig ....

2ND SKIER: No – no – no it would be best to start from the east and go zag-zag – zig-zig ....

They couldn't agree; the first skier decides to seek help from a resident nearby....

1ST SKIER: Excuse me sir, we are contemplating coming down the mountain tomorrow – do you think it would be best to go zag-zig or zag-zag – zig...?

RESIDENT: I can't help you ... I'm a tobogganist.

1ST SKIER: Oh well, in that case I'll have a packet of cigarettes and a box of matches ....

DES O'CONNOR

I have often tried to figure out why Des O'Connor has to take so much stick − if it's not from the media, it's from those who are far less talented − after all, Des looks good, his voice isn't a world beater but it is pleasant and he gives an enormous amount of pleasure with his TV shows − he brings a smile and, providing his guests are 'firing', he provides an hour's entertainment on his Tonight show that is usually as good as anything on the box, in many cases, far better.

I first became aware of Des in the early 1950s. I was fairly established in show business by then, having had a few recording successes, plus radio shows and being almost resident at the London Palladium. It was because of a letter I received, memorable for the sheer 'modesty' of the writer, Des.

I cannot remember it word for word because after I'd answered it, I tore it up − I wish I'd kept it but it was usual to receive half a dozen similar letters each week all on the same theme − 'Can you help me to get into show business?' Des kept the letter I sent him and told me he still has it to this very day.

I read his correspondence, which explained he was in the RAF serving his conscription but when he was released, he was going to try the entertainment business. He added that he sang a great deal better than I did − he told better jokes and that he was much better looking − what does he do with all this God-given talent? He asked, could I advise him how to start, where to find an agent and to look out because when he got going, he would unseat me from the perch I had and he would become the new Max Bygraves! I took time to write him a letter with the only advice I knew how to give, on the lines of 'learn to walk before you run – get audience experience – gather material – work in pantomimes and summer shows and don't be afraid to experiment'. I wished him good luck.

Several years later, our paths crossed and he introduced himself as the writer of the cheeky letter, but he had taken my advice and got a job as a redcoat at a Butlin's Holiday Camp. He thanked me and each time we meet he tells the story to anybody that cares to listen.

I was guesting on his Thames Television show not too long ago and the story of the letter and my reply came up. Des was telling it to some writers and camera men. I interrupted him to say, '...but Des, now you are established and a well-known name, surely you must get similar letters asking how to break into show biz, don't you?'

He confessed that he did. I asked him how he answered them. He got a big laugh when he told the assembled crew, 'I write back and say – get in touch with MAX BYGRAVES!'

KID: (Doing homework) Hey mum – how do lions make love?

MOTHER: I don't know, your father's a Rotarian!

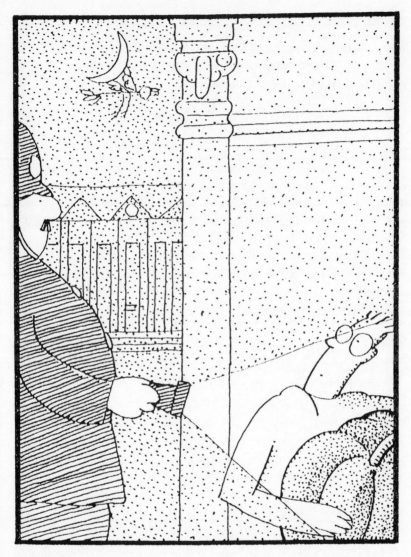

A policeman walking down the High Street shines his torch into a doorway and there on the floor is a fellow having a passionate affair with a pumpkin....

POLICEMAN: What are you doing:

FELLOW: Oh...has it gone twelve o'clock?

The guest speaker hadn't arrived for the Rotary Club luncheon so Rotarians drew lots among themselves on who would make the after dinner speech.

It is left to Charlie, who knows very little about speech-making but manages to keep his audience interested on the subject of *sex*. For twenty minutes, his theme is 'sex in fifty-seven ways'.

When he arrives home, his wife asks how the meeting went, he tells her that the guest speaker was delayed so *he* had to speak. 'What did you talk about? asks Charlie's wife. Not wishing her to know he talked about sex, he answered, 'Er...I talked about...er...SAILING'.

Next day, Charlie's wife is shopping and calls at the butcher's. The cheery butcher tells Charlie's wife that her man was brilliant at the meeting the day before. He added, 'He certainly knows his subject.'

His wife said, 'I'm surprised – he's only done it three times ... the first time his hat blew off ... the second time he was seasick ... and the third time the Navy had to lift him off with a helicopter!'

The two policemen in the patrol car rubbed their eyes as a car cruised by them at 80mph. They rubbed them again when they realised the driver was a middle-aged woman steering with her knees, knitting from a pattern propped up on the dashboard.

The nearside cop, after overtaking the lady, lowered the window and shouted 'Pull over!'

She smiled back, 'No – a pair of socks!'

A Scotsman had travelled from Glasgow to see his beloved
Scotland play England at Wembley but on the way he'd
lost his ticket. He approaches a ticket tout outside the
Stadium ....

SCOT: How much?

T.T.:   Hundred quid each.

SCOT: Hundred quid!!? In Scotland I could go to bed with a
        woman for that amount!

T.T.:   But you wouldn't get forty-five minutes each end and a
        brass band at half time, would yer?

SADIE: Sam – today you retire – come with me, I have a
        retirement present for you.

SAM: What is it, Sadie?

SADIE: Sit back in the car Sam – it's a surprise.

SAM: Sadie – I can't wait – please tell me ....

SADIE: Alright Sam – you see that small block of flats at
        the end of the road – they belong to us ....

SAM: What do you mean?

SADIE: Every time you made love to me, I put a few
        pounds away – for fifty years I did it and now we
        own that block of flats I bought with the money.

SAM: Sadie – why didn't you tell me before – I'd have
        given you *all* my business!

BOB DIXON

Bob Dixon was my accompanist for more than thirty-six years. He died a couple of years ago and I still can't get used to the idea that he is not behind me on stage appearances tinkling away at the piano.

We had a silent code going on between us: if an audience was not on our wavelength, I would switch channels – that is, go to a totally different routine to the one rehearsed. He would know I had changed gear and would be ready to play a piece that we hadn't performed for ten years or more, he had a photographic memory and could rattle off things like credits on an old movie – sometimes he'd remember who the make-up was done by.

He could do the *Times* crossword in half an hour and was an authority on sport, and he could drink – never before a show, but as soon as the curtain came down he would make the nearest bar faster than Sebastian Coe.

He came from Ulverston in Lancashire, although we travelled the length and breadth of Britain with twenty-odd trips around the world, he never lost his northern accent. In fact, it got more pronounced over the years.

A short rotund balding figure that earned him the nickname Mr Sheen, he was the most loyal and conscientious worker I have ever known. One thing he was not – was technically minded.

We were in Perth, Australia. I walked into his dressing room just before a show one evening and saw him getting ready to shave. His face was lathered and he was trying to fit a three holed blade into a safety razor he'd used back in his RAF days, twenty-five years before.

I told him he was wasting his time with that sort of razor – that there was a new plastic one on the market that was disposable. 'I'll get you some next time I go to the chemists'. A few days later, I bought a packet of half a dozen and gave them to him.

That same night, he walked into my dressing room and said, 'Them bloody razors wouldn't cut butter hot!' He still had the lather on his face, the razor in his hand. I looked at it and said, 'You have to take the orange plastic cover off before it works'. He had been trying to use it with the safety cover on.

After he had removed that and tried, he was more impressed. 'Where's the blade?' he asked, then ran his finger along the sharp edge to see. He cut his finger. It was only a small cut, but as he said at the time, 'I'm an easy bleeder'. We got one of the St John's ladies from the front of the theatre to try to stem the flow of blood but to no avail, we were 'on' in a few minutes.

My act usually lasts for more than an hour. When the curtain eventually came down, I walked over to the piano and there was blood all over the keyboard.

We had to get him to hospital, he even cancelled his journey to the bar. The blood kept flowing – it was one of the dancing girls that came up with an idea to stop the flow. She brought a large white improvised finger stall which seemed to stop the bleeding until we got him to hospital. In the car going to the infirmary he asked where the finger stall came from. It was hard to tell him that the device was what ladies use when that time of the month comes round.

We waited at the out-patients for a good hour or more; eventually the doctor, an uncouth young know-all who had been imbibing and was annoyed at being called for duty after midnight, staggered in and said to Bob, 'And what the hell's up with you?'

Bob bristled, held up his finger, and in broad Lancashire dialect, said, 'I'm 'aving a fooking period!'

My favourite political joke was when Reagan and Gorbachev first met.

REAGAN: Mr Gorbachev – what is that red mark on your forehead?

GORBACHEV: That? Oh that is a birthmark.

REAGAN: Really – how long have you had that?

A flash young punk rocker walks into a tattooist's and asks the tattooist to tattoo his testicles.

'Hang on...,' says the tattoo master, '...I'll get my ball pen!'

The men's barber was puzzled by a chap who poked his head into the shop each day to enquire, 'How long to wait?' The barber, who always had several customers at that time of day, would reckon up and say, 'Half an hour', or if very busy, 'At least an hour!'

After several weeks, the barber got curious and said to his assistant, 'There's a bloke puts his head in every day to ask how long to wait but he never comes back – tomorrow when he calls, put your coat on and follow him – see where he goes'.

Sure enough, next day, right on time, the enquirer asks, 'How long?' The barber tells him forty-five minutes and as he closes the door he tells the assistant to follow.

Five minutes later, the assistant returns.

BARBER: Did you follow him?

ASST.:   Yes.

BARBER: Where did he go?

ASST.:   Your house!

An Irishman walked into the dentist's office, bounced off the wall, fell on the floor, hit the ceiling, bounced off the door and landed in the chair....

DENTIST: Name please

PATIENT: Rick O'Shea

DENTIST: Welcome – I'm Phil McAvity!

GEOFF LOVE

For the obituary I wrote for the *Guardian* on Geoff Love (10 July 1991), the heading was 'Love – a many splendoured man'. I tried to put into words the deep affection and respect I had, and still have, for the lovely Geoff.

We first met in the early 1950s. In those days, Geoff was an arranger and I was recording for the HMV label. I was to record a song titled 'Meet Me on the Corner', a most successful top ten entry – we actually named a show after the title which had a long run at the London Hippodrome, now known as Stringfellows. The record was a hit equally because of Geoff's fine arrangement.

We met casually over the years, then in 1972 Thames TV asked me to appear in a series to be called simply *Max*. I was told I could have my choice of orchestras and, without hesitation, I plumped for Geoff Love. So started a partnership on TV that lasted over fifteen years.

This started in the days before the accountants became the top men in television, when we got paid for performing: nowadays the bottom line rules. The only appearance a performer is asked for now is to guest on a chat show, with the host who is picking up £5,000,000 per annum and the artiste can look forward to 'expenses'. In Australia it's even worse – not only are you expected to arrive under your own steam but to spend hours rehearsing – in make-up – provide your own material – and generally make the host look good – all for the 'plug'. I was having dinner earlier in the year with Ronnie Corbett and Danny La Rue and we were asking each other how Australian Equity permits this sort of racket – none of us had an answer.

Back to Geoff, who had trouble rolling his Rs. For our back-chat, the writers, unknown to Geoff would write a line full of Rs, like: 'The Rolls-Royce is round on the ramp'. When Geoff delivered the line, it came out, 'The Wolls-Woyce is wound on the wamp!' Sometimes, to get an extra laugh, I'd say, 'Geoff, would you mind *w*epeating that'.

Geoff also recorded as Manuel of the Mountains; his records sold in large numbers down Argentina way. He provided backings for Shirley Bassey, Russ Conway and many more top recording stars. In between, he gave his time to Stars Organisation for Spastics (SOS).

His happiest days were spent in Spain where he was water skiing up to a short time before his death.

When work permitted, he would get into his Jaguar with his lovely wife Joyce and snatch a few days at Sitges, south of Barcelona. He'd return and show off his suntan, the grandson of a Cherokee Indian it was hard to see but he assured us it was there, even Joyce a born and bred English lady, would shake her head in disbelief.

On one of his last trips to Spain he was mugged, it happened just outside Lyons in France. He was flagged down by a 'conman' in another car. When Geoff stopped, he pointed to his back wheel Geoff got out to see what was wrong – an accomplice jumped in the driving seat, turned the key which Geoff had left in and was away with the Jaguar, plus all Geoff's belongings, passport, money, etc.

Geoff was telling me all this over the phone when he arrived back in England. 'I don't suppose you will feel like going back to Spain again, will you Geoff?' I asked.

'Oh yes...' he replied, '... I don't feel the same without a tan'.

Two Jewish ladies are talking....

SARAH: Hey Rachel – you know Mr Solomons across the road – the one with the big car and the penthouse – on Saturday night he has invited me out to dinner.

RACHEL: Two weeks ago – I went out with him – I'll tell you what happens: his chauffeur picks you up in the car – you go to the Savoy Hotel – such a dinner you've never had – caviare – smoked salmon – Dom Perignon champagne – the lot! On the way home, he asks would I like to go to his penthouse for a drink – I agree, we arrive. As I turn round, he's locking the door – he walks towards me – he's a changed man – he's an animal – he rips off my dress – he carries me into his bedroom and mauls me passionately for more than an hour!

SARAH: Do you think I should go!

RACHEL: Go? Of course go – but wear an old dress.

The night before the wedding

Oh what a night of shenanigans
Before Micky Flanagan wed
He was lying there sleeping peacefully
When they slipped something into his bed
It was an inflatable woman, perfect in every way
With long blonde hair and a smile in her eyes
That could steal your heart away.

The next day the boys said 'Micky –
How did you enjoy your last fling –
Did you like the girl we put in your bed
Come tell us now everything'.
'Well,' Micky said, ' I am surprised now
She was lying there begging for more
But when I bit her ear – she just went zzzzzzzzzzz
And flew right out the door!'

As I approached a group of workmen outside my flat in London recently, one said, 'Oi, Max – you let us down.' I couldn't understand what he meant. 'How do you mean – I let you down?'

The spokesman for the workers said, 'When Frankie Howerd and Benny Hill died – we had you down for a treble!'